Minibeasts Matter!

Claire Llewellyn

Explorer Challenge

Find out what this minibeast eats ...

OXFORD
UNIVERSITY PRESS

Contents

I Like Minibeasts 4

Minibeasts Look Fantastic! 6

This Minibeast Makes Honey 8

Minibeasts Make Better Soil 10

Minibeasts Get Rid of Pests 12

Minibeasts Spread Pollen 14

Minibeasts Clear Up Rubbish 16

Minibeasts Are Food 18

Minibeasts Matter! 20

Glossary and Index 22

Look Back, Explorers 23

I Like Minibeasts

I like minibeasts. These small animals are important and help us in many ways.

Did you know?
There are millions of
different kinds of minibeast.

Some people don't like minibeasts.
I think they're wrong. Here are seven reasons
why minibeasts are the BEST!

Minibeasts Look Fantastic!

Let's look at some minibeasts close up.

This beetle looks like it's made of gold.

You can see through this dragonfly's wings.

This moth has beautiful wings with spots that look like eyes.

Did you know?

A dragonfly's eyes cover most of its head.

Every minibeast is different.

Aren't they fantastic?

This Minibeast Makes Honey

If you eat honey, you'll like this minibeast. It's the honeybee!

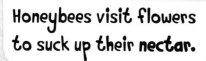

Honeybees visit flowers to suck up their **nectar.**

Honeybees collect the **nectar** and take it back to the nest. There they turn it into honey. They feed on the honey in the winter.

a bees' nest

Did you know?
Honeybees visit over two million flowers to make one jar of honey.

Minibeasts Make Better Soil

Many worms live under the ground. They burrow through the soil, and help to break it up. This makes it easier for plants to grow in the soil.

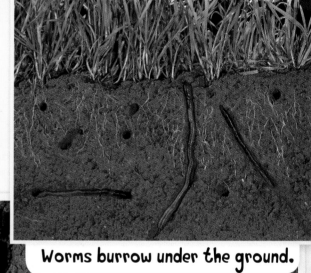

Worms burrow under the ground.

There may be more than two million worms in a field the size of a football pitch.

Minibeasts Get Rid of Pests

Pests spoil plants and crops. Farmers and gardeners like minibeasts that feed on pests.

Minibeasts eat all sorts of pests.

This spider catches pests in a web.

Did you know?
A hungry ladybird eats about 100 greenfly a day.

13

Minibeasts Spread Pollen

When a butterfly lands on a flower,
it picks up a yellow dust called **pollen**.

It spreads pollen from flower to flower.
The pollen helps the plants to make seeds.

Butterflies feed on flowers.

pollen

Did you know?

Bees, wasps and moths spread pollen too.

15

Minibeasts Clear Up Rubbish

What happens to food scraps and rotting plants and dead animals? Minibeasts help to clear them up. They make the world a cleaner place.

Some slugs and snails feed on rotting wood or fruit.

Did you know?

Slugs and snails have rows of tiny teeth to shred their food.

Minibeasts Are Food

Many animals feed on minibeasts. Fish, frogs, mice and birds feed on **insects**, worms and slugs.

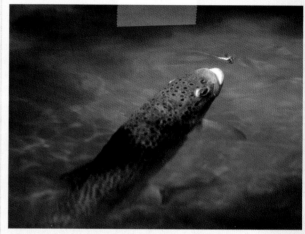

Then bigger hunters, such as owls, sharks and bears eat the fish, frogs, mice and birds.

Did you know?
Many people around the world eat grasshoppers, **grubs** and snails.

Minibeasts Matter!

There are good reasons
to like minibeasts.

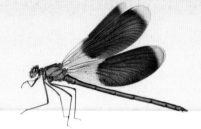

They look amazing.

They make honey.

They make better soil.

They get rid of pests.

They spread pollen.

They clear up rubbish.

They are an
important food.

Minibeasts matter.
Don't you agree?

Glossary

grub: tiny creature that hatches from an insect's egg; it will become an insect

insect: animal with six legs, like a butterfly, bee or ant

nectar: sweet liquid inside a flower

pest: animal that spoils plants and crops

pollen: yellow dust inside flowers

Index

bee	8-9, 15
butterfly	14-15
flower	8-9, 14-15
pollen	14-15, 20
slug	16-17, 18
snail	16-17
spider	13
worm	10-11, 18

Look Back, Explorers

How does a spider catch pests?

How many flowers do honeybees visit to make one jar of honey?

Can you give two reasons why minibeasts are the best?

One beetle looks like it is 'made of gold'. What other words would you use to describe it?

Did you find out what this minibeast eats?

What's Next, Explorers?

Now you have read about minibeasts, go on a magic key adventure with Biff, Chip and Kipper to see what minibeasts they find in the Australian bush ...

Grub Up

Series created by Roderick Hunt and Alex Brychta

OXFORD

Explorer Challenge
for *Grub Up*

Find out what minibeast this bird meets ...